MW01093445

LETTERS TO A PERFECTIONIST

On Shame, Fear, Love, and the Surprising Spiritual Nature of Perfectionism

---

TAD FRIZZELL

Lucky Jack Productions LLC

Dedication

This book is dedicated to all of my teachers: my family, my spiritual mentors, friends and especially to A., who told me "you have to write."

My beloved spoke, and said to me:

"Rise up, my love, my fair one,

And come away.

For lo, the winter is past,

The rain is over *and* gone.

The flowers appear on the earth;

The time of singing has come..."

Song of Solomon 2:10-12a

Contents

Preface

The phenomenon of perfectionism and its increasing impact on the lives of both young and old in our times is a popular topic of discussion today. If the word *holistic* is taken to mean "a comprehension of the parts of something as intimately inter-connected and explicable only by reference to the whole," then it's a word that applies perfectly to the phenomenon of perfec-tionism and its associated problems. The symptoms presented by a suffering perfectionist usually include depression, anxiety, obsessive-compulsive disorders, eating disorders, substance abuse, self-harm and suicide, in some combination. Any one of these symptoms is destructive enough to pose a serious threat to a person's well-being.

If the phenomenon of perfectionism is by nature *holistic*, so must be the understanding and the cure. Perfectionism is a tree with a spiritual root, and only by digging deep to find its essence can we begin to understand the fruit of perfectionism. The fruit which this tree produces changes over time as a person continues to engage perfectionism as a way of being. What may seem in childhood to be a tendency for high achievement combined with some quirky behaviors and intense displays of emotion can grow through adulthood into a serious spiritual illness with enough psychological symptoms to bring a person's life to a halt. Based on my experience of this progression, I believe it is essential for perfectionists and their loved ones alike (especially parents) to become aware and to act. People often "make a deal" with perfectionism at some point in childhood in order to achieve more and meet their need for security without counting the cost.

Everyone wants to change their experience of life in some way, but for suffering perfectionists the desire to change their experience of life is not a whimsical one. Left unchecked, perfectionism (because of its spiritual nature) has a way of taking over the mind and the heart to such a degree that life becomes a dreary march through a dark swamp. New knowledge is necessary for new experience, and what is required here is self-knowledge. We may acquire this self knowledge in one of two ways. One way is through intense suffering and subsequent reflection. The other is through sharing and introspection. I am sharing the self-knowledge I acquired through intense suffering and subsequent reflection in hopes that wherever you are in your "arc" of perfectionism, you might become aware of the dangers and avert a personal disaster. These letters represent a no-holds-barred look at the most rotten fruits of the tree of perfectionism on one hand, and a holistic approach to a new way of being on the other.

As dreary as the march through the dark swamp of perfectionism might be, there are hidden treasures to be found along the way. The journey we take through the door of self-knowledge on the way to healing opens other doors which were once closed to us. Not only will we discover the inner workings of our mind and heart and learn to embrace our true identity, we will come into contact with a love we never knew existed. A love which replaces shame, informs our every action, and returns to us our sense of wonder. Hidden in this love is a great paradox. How do we know when we have arrived at this love? Precisely when we reach a state of deep gratitude for the perfectionism which both blocked us from finding this love earlier, and through suffering and self-knowledge delivered it to us whole. I wish you patience, perseverance, and enlightenment on the journey.

* * *

A note on gender: Because the following letters are written as if to one specific person, I have consistently used masculine-gendered pronouns throughout. Nevertheless, I consider all of the phenomena I describe to be universal and not exclusive to gender.

Letter One: The Surprising Spiritual Nature of Perfectionism

DEAR BELOVED,

People are talking a lot about perfectionism today. It's a phenomenon which is causing a lot of pain, and they're looking for solutions. I did some checking, and found that there are around 12,000 combined online searches per month for the words "perfectionism" and "perfectionist." Those who study mental health are noticing that many people today are afflicted with not one but a complex of problems including depression, anxiety, obsessive-compulsive disorder, body-image and eating disorders. When the pain becomes unbearable these suffering souls often try to numb the pain with drugs, alcohol, and self-harm. For some the end result is suicide. The same psychologists and therapists are now more frequently associating this complex of symptoms (all serious in their own right) with a root cause, and calling it *perfectionism*.

Perfectionism has been defined by the psychological community as a personality trait characterized by the personal striving for the state of perfection. In the midst of this striving the perfectionist tends to set unreasonable goals and attempts compulsively and obsessively to achieve these goals. The perfectionist measures his self-worth externally, by how much is accomplished–and the amount of time this accomplishment takes. Because the goals are unreasonable and impossible to reach, the perfectionist naturally fails to meet his own expectations, and in this way arrives at a very low estimation of self-worth. That's when the symptoms and side effects begin to manifest and cause a ripple effect in the life of the perfectionist.

But that is not all. You see, perfectionism is a spiritual problem. I don't mean that it is a religious problem (though it can be). The word "spiritual" can mean many different things depending on the context in which it is used. I am using the word according to the most basic definition. A spiritual problem is a problem which burdens every aspect of our being–mind and body, heart and soul. Perfectionism is just such a problem. It's much more than a way of thinking. It's a way of being, a way of relating to ourselves and the world around us. It's a *holistic* problem which requires a *holistic* approach. Treating the individual symptoms just won't do.

I came up with my own definition of perfectionism which I believe is helpful if we are to touch the very soul of perfectionism: **the refusal to love and accept oneself in a state of imperfection**. Every perfectionist knows that this definition is the truest and most profound, as it touches on the spiritual nature of perfectionism. Of course, we could leave off the words "in a state of imperfection" from the definition. On one hand they seem a little silly, don't they? Everyone knows that there is no perfection in this life. Or do they? These words make the point quite well. Perfectionists secretly believe that perfection is just down the road a little and waiting for their best effort. We perfectionists are willing to deprive ourselves of our own love and acceptance until this elusive goal is finally reached. When we do this day after day and year after year, the cost of our refusal to love and accept ourselves grows. Unchecked and untreated, this refusal can cost us our very life.

When we refuse to love ourselves, we also refuse to believe that God or any other person could possibly love us the way we are. We set up barriers to love. These barriers don't just prevent love from accessing our heart. They make the heart as dry as a desert. Just as the desert has no water to offer, so we also have no love to offer our fellow travelers on the road of life. Without love, the heart withers.

In the next letter I will tell you how I learned about the true nature of perfectionism through many years of painful experience. For now, please tell me if what I have written here is true in your own life.

YOURS,

Tad

Letter Two: How I Learned about Perfectionism the Hard Way

DEAR BELOVED,

I promised to tell you how I learned about perfectionism. It took me a long time to name the problem for myself. Remember, I am using my definition for perfectionism: **the refusal to love and accept oneself in a state of imperfection**. For me, this definition touches on the spiritual nature of perfectionism. In my experience this is a deeply spiritual matter. The definition applies universally, no matter the creed or culture.

There was a time in my life when I thought I was just highly-driven and overly serious. My parents noticed early that I was always very hard on myself. This frightened them, and they tried to protect me from outside pressures. There was plenty of pressure inside. No additional pressure was needed to motivate me. When I got serious about a sport, I set up my training like a professional would, even at the age of 14. I was habitually setting unrealistic goals for myself. I was often crushed when I inevitably failed to reach these goals. But I kept doing the same thing, over and over again. For the sake of perfection and rapid improvement in sport I even developed an eating disorder for a time.

Sometimes perfectionism was my best friend. It made me unsatisfied in a way that drove me to do and experience more than I ever would have otherwise. This innate drive led to many wonderful adventures. It was easy for me to become obsessed, and one of my obsessions was with mountains. Perfectionism helped me to prepare well for my unforgettable adventures in those mountains. But when my desire to control everything was applied to my relationships, the results were tragic. Confused about my habit of driving others (especially girlfriends) away, I eventually applied my perfectionism to another aspect of my life which had always been important to me—the spiritual life. Understanding myself and others was too difficult. What I really needed (or so I thought) was to find the perfect system for getting as close to God as possible. As quickly as possible. I left everything and entered a monastery. I was 25 years old.

Sixteen years later I found myself burned out, disillusioned, physically sick, and with the symptoms of a broken brain. The problem wasn't the monastery. All my wounds were self-inflicted. Finding prayer and real spiritual work difficult, I gravitated toward the physical work and practical matters. As we were building a monastery from scratch on a mountain in Appalachia, the list of projects was endless. I served as a priest and administrator, traveled extensively on monastery business and pilgrimages, and year by year took on more responsibilities and more stress. I multitasked from early morning to late at night with computers, cell-phones, two-way radios and personal conversations—always on high-alert. We experienced three building fires, countless floods, landslides and the usual "people problems" that come with life in community. Around the time I turned 40 years old, I cracked. When I finally paused to take stock of what had happened to me, I realized something. I had spent all these years reading and speaking about the love of God, but I had refused to accept such a love, or to love and care for myself. I had been trying to please people, multiple authority figures who often didn't agree with each other about what I should be devoting my energy to. I didn't know who I was anymore. I had been running after perfection, and trying to control everything in an effort to meet my need for security. The pride of perfectionism is no foundation on which to build a spiritual life. What's required is humility. I was motivated by the shame of never being enough, and the fear of failure and criticism. I had followed the arc of perfectionism to its furthest point. Almost.

In a future letter I will tell you how my experience with perfectionism continued, even if the circumstances of my life changed the day I left the monastery with the blessing of the superior.

Of course, there is much more to my life than this experience of perfectionism. My life has been full of magic, music, poetry, friends, and beautiful sunrises in wild places. But this perfectionism, my refusal to love and accept myself in a state of imperfection, has been like a strong undertow which always pulled me under. It informed my actions and reactions. Until I observed it, named it, studied it, and set out to transform it, it overshadowed everything.

I'm sure the circumstances of your life are very different from mine. But do you see a collection of symptoms and side effects causing you pain and confusion? Depression, anxiety, the impulse to control, disgust with yourself, the burden of shame, obsessive or compulsive behaviors? Perhaps eating disorders, attempts to numb the pain, or even a desire to harm yourself? Is perfectionism—the refusal to love and accept yourself in a state of imperfection—the root of all these symptoms? I would encourage you to name it.

In the next letter I would like to explain how we experience perfectionism first as a friend, and later as an enemy.

YOURS,

Tad

Letter Three: The Pervasive Nature of Perfectionism

DEAR BELOVED,

Here is the problem with perfectionism. First we begin to use it to obtain positive results, exert control over ourselves and our environment, and become better human beings. Then it takes on a life of its own and begins to control us. The reason for this lies in its spiritual nature. At some point, it becomes not just a tool we *use* but a way of being. That may sound simple, but when we talk about *a way of being* we are touching on a complex web of forces inside us. We are talking about the expectations we set for ourselves, the way we treat (and talk to) ourselves when we don't meet those expectations, the forces that motivate us, and the strategies we use to meet our human needs. Once all of these forces are set in motion, we can't help but live in a certain kind of energy, and share that energy with the world around us. That's when perfectionism is no longer restricted to the area of our life where we first used its power and it begins to affect our work, our relationships, and our spiritual life.

Let's remind ourselves of the definition of perfectionism we have agreed on: **the refusal to love and accept oneself in a state of imperfection.** Let's begin by taking an inventory of our life. You can join me in asking some important questions:

- Am I setting unrealistic expectations for myself, then beating myself up when I don't meet them?
- Is my frustration at not being able to fully control myself and the world around me growing steadily over time, leading to more and more anxiety and depression?
- Am I dealing with my growing anxiety by behaving more and more compulsively?
- Am I dealing with the pain of depression by looking for something to numb the pain?
- Are my relationships suffering because I am too hard on myself and on others?
- Am I motivated solely by shame and fear in everything I do (and fail to do)?
- Have I reached such a level of self-hatred that I am losing my sense of identity, trying to create a new persona and mimicking those whom I perceive to be more lovable and likable than me?
- Is my refusal to love and accept myself in a state of imperfection poisoning every aspect of my life?
- And for some people: Has my image of God morphed into that of a brutal taskmaster? Am I burdened by the shame of not living up to a standard of spiritual perfection I have imagined to be necessary to make myself worthy of God's love and mercy?

At the end of the road, when perfectionism was literally threatening my will to live, I would have answered yes to all of the above. But it wasn't always that way. Perfectionism took over my life slowly, year by year. It started in childhood, but it was at first only applied to athletic pursuits. I did tend to take things a lot more seriously than others my age. Certain decisions I made sped up the pace at which perfectionism pervaded every aspect of my life. In my ignorance, I tried to solve the problems created by perfectionism by applying more perfectionism.

Everyone is different. But from experience I am sure of one thing: unchecked and untreated, perfectionism has a way of taking control of more and more of our life until it seriously threatens our well-being. Wherever you are in your journey, I encourage you to pause now. Assess the affects of your refusal to love and accept yourself in a state of imperfection. It may seem to you now that perfectionism is something you control and make use of when you like. If you don't proceed carefully, it may soon control you.

YOURS,

Tad

Letter Four: The Perfectionist Filter

DEAR BELOVED,

Let's break down the way a perfectionist experiences life moment by moment. We will focus on thoughts and emotions, the two basic components of our experience of life.

As the perfectionist takes in information it passes through what I call the *perfectionist filter*, and that is where the information is distorted. When we look at one psychological problem closely related to perfectionism—body dysmorphic disorder—we see this distortion in action. The perfectionist with this particular disorder looks in the mirror and sees something ugly and grotesque. As human beings we grow accustomed to trusting our brain, but it can play tricks on us.

Modern brain science is developing rapidly, and our understanding of the interaction between the mind and the body is becoming more evolved with each passing year. The nervous system and the chemicals which facilitate the functions of the mind and body are being tested and studied like never before. This knowledge can help us in our understanding of perfectionism, and why it is more than just a way of thinking. What are some of the most common thoughts associated with perfectionism?

- I am a failure.
- I am useless.
- I am worthless.
- I haven't accomplished enough today / this week / this year / in my life.
- I am not reaching my goals fast enough.
- I am fat / ugly.
- People are not happy with me.
- People expect more from me.
- People won't love me unless I get this right.

And for some people:

- God is not happy with me.
- God expects more from me.
- God won't love me unless I become perfect.

It turns out that when we have a thought, our body experiences that thought as emotion, through the work of neurotransmitters and hormones. What are some of the most common emotions associated with these thoughts?

- Sadness
- Anger
- Fear

- Frustration
- Disgust
- Anxiety

When the body becomes accustomed to the "signature" of a given thought—an emotion—this combination of thought and emotion takes the form of a habit. If the thought and the emotion are destructive, the habit takes on the character of an illness.

We can confirm this by looking at our own experience. The relationship between these thoughts and emotions is cyclical. We think we are worthless, so we feel sad. The sadness settles in to our body and becomes a habit of feeling, encouraging more of the same thoughts. In other words, the thoughts nourish the emotion in the body and the emotion in the body nourishes the thoughts. For the perfectionist, the thoughts and emotions listed above follow this very process. That's how perfectionism becomes a spiritual illness. We think of the heart as the spiritual center of the body, which is why we say things like "she died of a broken heart," or "my heart is overflowing." For our purposes, we will consider that the heart is where the illness resides, though the toxins are distributed throughout the mind and body.

We can consider thoughts as the food which we offer to the body through the work of neurotransmitters and hormones. Common sense tells us that if we nourish our body with the same food today that we did yesterday, we will get the same results. That is, we will arrive at the same emotions which will then feed those emotions back to the mind, encouraging the mind to produce more of the same thoughts. If the "food" we offer to the body is destructive, the emotions will be destructive as well.

As fascinating as the findings of modern brain science are, they are only revealing the chemistry and mechanics of the processes which students of the human soul, mind, and body have known and taught for centuries. People dedicated to the science of the spiritual life observed themselves in extended prayer and meditation, and came to the same conclusions long ago.

The perfectionist filter doesn't allow in the positive thoughts that create positive emotions. The only thoughts that pass through this filter are thoughts of disappointment, self-criticism, and failure. Yet somehow we think that by being harder on ourselves we will eventually accomplish more and become perfect. The reality is that the emotions which are created by these thoughts and contribute to more of the same won't allow that. When this process takes root in childhood, the habits of thought and emotion can be hard to break. Such an illness is not easy to cure, but it can be done. We have to start with the place where the illness began.

YOURS,

Tad

Letter Five: The Perfectionist Child and the Child Inside the Perfectionist

DEAR BELOVED,

I remember the day it all began to change for the better. It was the day I finally heard the voice inside. I had already followed the arc of perfectionism to what I thought was its furthest point, burned out severely, changed the circumstances of my life drastically, and in many ways lived differently. But when a series of events left me disoriented and grasping for my old strategy of control, I first panicked–then promptly broke my ankle. People fall ill or break a bone all the time, but for me it was a sign and an opportunity. I was suddenly immobile, alone, and growing more depressed by the day. I hate to sit still. It's easier for me to keep running than to sit and face myself. The message was clear. I still had something—or perhaps *someone*—important to visit deep within myself. It was then that I heard the voice of the poor and abandoned child, buried under 42 years of perfectionism, crying out to me for attention. That's the day I understood the problem and named it. Up until that day I had simply refused to love and accept myself in a state of imperfection. Which means I had refused to love and accept myself at all. That abandoned, unloved child inside must have noticed his greatest opportunity in the form of a broken ankle, and he was bound and determined to finally get my attention.

Have you ever had the feeling that at some point in your life, you stopped treating yourself as a friend, and began to scold yourself mercilessly every time you made a small mistake? For most of us perfectionists, this happened in childhood.

Like me, you may have noticed something. Some people seem to be born with a capacity for self-compassion and self-acceptance. Genes probably play a role—some say they make up 50% of who we are. Education certainly affects our development. Family systems and invisible influences have a way of shaping us which can be mysterious until therapy reveals the forces at work. Just because self-love comes naturally for some people doesn't mean they are destined to coddle themselves and achieve nothing. It just means that they mix their strivings with care for themselves, and when the results of their strivings are less than perfect, they mix self-criticism with self-soothing.

We perfectionists don't do that. Perhaps we are afraid that if we are too kind to ourselves we will achieve nothing. Whatever the case, when the refusal to love and accept ourselves in a state of imperfection becomes a way of life, we become experts at violent self-criticism and never run out of reasons to punish ourselves. Our methods for punishment, and our tactics for numbing the pain of self-hatred grow and evolve with time. This way of being doesn't change easily, no matter what age we are when we recognize the problem and choose a new way.

When we begin to treat ourselves this way in our childhood, that child inside who only wants our love, attention, care, and respect retreats into a corner somewhere. He hides, fearing another beating. In a way, our childhood is cut short and we lose our sense of wonder. We forget how to play, and how to enjoy life.

As we perfectionists grow up, we become our own private and ever-present bully. Perfectionism is the voice of the accuser. When we pay attention to what perfectionism says to us, we notice that it is always accusing us of something. Of not being enough, of being a failure, of bringing shame on ourselves and those around us. You know exactly what I mean. When we as children with perfectionist tendencies become aware of the great gulf between ourselves and perfection, we do the only thing we can think of to bridge the gap: achieve well and achieve quickly. That's when the unrealistic expectations come into play.

YOURS,

Tad

Letter Six: Unrealistic Expectations

DEAR BELOVED,

Some of us have to learn the hard way. And some of us have to learn the hard way, forget what we learned, and learn it again hundreds of times. That's what a perfectionist's struggle with unrealistic goals and expectations feels like. We often experience a certain euphoria as we are beginning a new project, because we see the landscape of possibilities spread wide before us. Inside every neurotic perfectionist is a hopeful dreamer, an overachiever who is striving for something more than the "usual stuff" his native environment has to offer. It would be a beautiful thing if it remained that simple.

Unfortunately, the euphorically hopeful perfectionist often sits down and makes a list of goals for his new project which are completely unrealistic. I've done it myself thousands of times. Sitting and looking at an impressive list of goals complete with the dates by which I will achieve them, I feel quite satisfied. Until the moment when things like unexpected events, a case of the flu, or just plain old bad days come into the picture. But this recipe for future disappointment is one part pride and one part denial, with a dash of self-hatred waiting for the right moment to enter the mix. Goal-setting is but one example of how we perfectionists tend to "poison the well," taking something which is meant to be constructive and turning it into something destructive. The practice of goal-setting is meant to foster success. But when we place enormous burdens on ourselves, then savagely beat ourselves for not being able to bear them, we are sabotaging any chance of success.

Real perfectionists know the great paradox that is always working in their assumptions: the perfectionist is filled with an inflated sense of his ability, and a sentiment bordering on self-hatred–all at the same time. Wanting so much to finally do something that will finally make me worthy of love and acceptance, I set the scene:

> *"You can do it this time! Set those unrealistic goals, forget all the practical realities you faced in the past. You really can go without sleep, work 16 hours every day (even on weekends), exercise three hours every day and skip dinner every night to make it all happen. Just think about the speed at which you will accomplish your work, and how many pounds you will lose in the process. Forget about what happened last time, and the time before that. Surely nothing will happen that would require you to add even a few more days to your timeline. Onward, Superman!"*

Everyone falls short of their goals from time to time, even people who set reasonable goals and don't behave as perfectionists. Missing the mark is part of life as a human being. For perfectionists however, the stakes are high. When the weight doesn't come off the way we expect, and the circumstances of life slow us down a bit, we begin beating ourselves up. We have just done it again—set ourselves up for failure, failed miserably, taken the measurement our self-worth and given ourselves a score of zero—and descended into that dark and dreary swamp of self-criticism.

The damage we do here is actually two-fold. On one hand we set ourselves up for failure by setting unrealistic goals, or simply giving ourselves far too little time to achieve them. On the other hand, we deprive ourselves of the possibility of celebrating our little victories. Little victories, like milestones along the path toward a greater goal, are an important part of the journey and we need to celebrate them. Perfectionists find it hard to recognize these milestones, and usually refuse to celebrate even these minor accomplishments. When I finally burned out, I looked back only to realize that I never celebrated anything. I accomplished many things, but I always moved on to the next project immediately without taking a moment for celebration. My black hole of perfectionism, that refusal to love and accept myself, could never be filled.

Withholding love from ourselves as we work towards our goals usually manifests as a tragic lack of self-care. Depending on what our goals are, this could mean depriving ourselves of sleep, nutrition, exercise, downtime, time for spiritual practice, or meaningful interactions with others.

For now, let's admit that this is the process we repeat again and again in our lives as perfectionists. Recognizing and admitting this habit is one step toward a new way of being.

Unrealistic expectations don't just harm my relationship with myself. They profoundly affect my relationships with others. That will be the subject of the next letter.

YOURS,

Tad

Letter Seven: Strained Relationships

DEAR BELOVED,

We're not finished talking about unrealistic expectations. We don't just have unrealistic expectations for ourselves, we have them for others. If it was only my living space that needed to be perfectly clean and ordered, disinfected and sparkling, my body that needed to be perfectly shaped and rocking the ideal body mass index, perhaps the damage could be contained. But unless we have really begun to work with ourselves to trim back the perfectionism which is bleeding over into our relationships like ink in a malfunctioning printer, we have a problem in the area of relationships as well.

When our perfectionism is entrenched and unchecked, it can be hard for us to remember that not everyone shares our values. The world is full of people who enjoy life, go with the flow, eat the things that are on our "bad list" and let the trash bin spill out onto the ground. And they like it that way. They might also have a great deal more self-compassion than we do, a healthy level of self-acceptance, and a lower level of stress than we have. Not every person will wash the dishes just the way we believe they should be washed, but they might have a great deal of wisdom to share with us while the washing is done. Sadly, we miss that wisdom and many other rich and valuable moments that make life beautiful when we are caught up in the details and chained to our unrealistic expectations for others.

Unrealistic expectations can damage friendships, isolate people within even the most loving family, and erode the relationship between spouses or partners. In my experience, we perfectionists tend to push it right up to the limit. We push and harass with both verbal and nonverbal communication until we see that we have irritated someone. Then we back off a little, but as our behavior is so often appropriately described as obsessive and compulsive, we can't control ourselves and begin again a short time later. In extreme cases, we can even reach a level of total insensitivity. Then we violently advocate for our way of doing and seeing things. We are attached to our way of being, and unable to consider another approach to life.

We perfectionists often make a crucial error when we enter into a relationship. *We* may have signed a contract with ourselves to strive unceasingly for perfection. That doesn't mean others have signed the same contract. Instead of approaching a relationship with someone else as a celebration of the uniqueness of each human being, and the acceptance of another human being "just as they are," we tend to imagine that in desiring a relationship with us they are joining us in the pursuit of perfection. It's a form of *assumption*. Maybe it's also a form of *projection*. We experience many different kinds of relationships as we move through life—coworker, employee, boss, spouse, parent, leader, and follower—and if this assumption is the foundation for each of those relationships, there's bound to be trouble.

What happens when we repeatedly hold to unrealistic expectations for ourselves and others? We learn the perfectionist's formula for motivation.

YOURS,

Tad

Letter Eight: What Motivates Perfectionists

DEAR BELOVED,

What if everyone, in every place and at every time were motivated only by love? What if love were the driving force behind every movement of the mind, body, and soul of every human being that ever walked the earth? It's a utopian dream, but it makes for a great thought experiment. The complex system of laws, rules, and punishments that have been employed since the dawn of civilization to keep society from completely breaking apart reveals the truth: we don't trust ourselves or others to be motivated purely by love.

That's what made Jesus Christ so revolutionary, and what made him so irritating to the Pharisees (the self-righteous) of his day. He proposed a new way of being, one based on the Law of Love–and made himself the first example. Just how difficult the Gospel of Love was for mankind to grasp is revealed in the centuries which followed. The Church (especially when emperors got involved) multiplied over time the number of rules and laws which it applies to the faithful. The Christian Church is by no means the only organized religion which has followed this pattern. In fact, you would be hard-pressed to find any organization, religious or otherwise, which *reduces* the number of laws and rules as it evolves over time. The truth is that when confronted with the dark side of human nature it's frightening to put your hope in love as a motivating force and much easier to govern people through laws and rules. Why does humanity behave in this way and not another? It's precisely because fear and shame are powerful motivators. This is universally true, even if codices of laws and rules do often arise from a loving entity with pure intent.

No one knows the power of shame and fear better than the perfectionist. But depending on where you are in your journey with perfectionism, you might not have realized it. You might not have become *conscious* of the forces which motivate you to the point of consuming your life. Take a look at your actions and reactions in the days, weeks, months, and years past. What motivated you? What motivates you now?

Love certainly can be a motivating force, even the greatest of all motivators. Saints and spiritual heroes fascinate us and capture our hearts simply because through love they seemed to conquer the world and soften even the hardest of hearts. For perfectionists however, there is a fundamental problem. The lack of healthy self-love closes the door to this great motivating force. This lack also corrodes and corrupts our ability to love others. Why is this so?

When love as a motivating force is not an option, the perfectionist quickly learns to use the other motivating forces of shame and fear. We could actually call them anti-motivators, and they are untrustworthy partners. It's not that they don't do their job. It's just that once we have enlisted their services we can easily lose control of their power. Before we realize what's happening, shame and fear take over our lives. They greet us as we open our eyes in the morning, follow us through the day, and haunt us at night. Once our mind recognizes the tremendous power shame and fear have over us, it suggests that we make use of them to motivate others as well. That's how our relationships become toxic.

Shame is that deep sense of unworthiness, that gnawing feeling that we never have been and never will be enough. It's the deep conviction that we have nothing to offer to the world, even though we try to please. It only motivates us by threatening us with more of itself. It never motivates us to *rest* or *celebrate*, only to *do*, even to do *great things*. But when it's present, it makes the doing burdensome. In contrast, love makes things light and easy. When it comes to energy, shame is a vampire and love is an artesian well, a fountain overflowing.

Fear is the voice which tells us that anything less than perfect will not be tolerated. It's the force behind our procrastination, because we fear that voice is telling the truth, that it really is better to keep to ourselves than to risk criticism. Some people use it to keep us where we are, in a place where we are useful to them. We can't blame them. Every one of us wants our needs met, and we use strategies to meet them. We are all a part of someone's strategy to meet a need, and others are certainly a part of our own.

As my perfectionistic journey reached its lowest valley, I realized that my habit of being motivated by shame and fear had become so entrenched that it defined my way of being in the world. It also distorted my image of God. I saw the law of attraction in action. Since I motivated myself to action (or inaction at times because of fear) by feeling ashamed for not being perfect, I attracted people who were very skilled at using shame and fear to motivate others to meet their needs. I really don't think they were even aware of this. Perhaps they were just like me—caught in the trap of motivating themselves in the same way. I do know that I eventually learned the system well. I took the shame and fear which pushed me from behind and made use of it to motivate others. I was a master of the guilt-trip, and easily mastered by it. There's no question that it works most of the time, since the world is full of people who are burdened by the same anti-motivators, even if they are not perfectionists. Every once in a while however, you encounter people with enough self-compassion and gathered wisdom, such that they create healthy boundaries around their hearts and minds and refuse to play the game. It's interesting to observe the behavior of Jesus when he encountered the masters of shame, the Pharisees, as recorded in the Gospels. He foiled their attempts to shame him and the people around him every time. Why? Because he knew only one motivating force—the force of love. It's not that he never scolded anyone. It's just that he only scolded those who transgressed against unconditional love, those who used fear and shame to wield power over others.

When it comes to shame, the perfectionist's experience can become quite complicated. At a certain point we realize that our perfectionism is *itself* a problem, and an irritant to others. Then we become ashamed not only of our imperfection, but ashamed of our perfectionism as well. We try to hide it. Depending on the level of our acting ability, we might be able to fool others into thinking we are content, well-adjusted, and able to go with the flow. But acting is a far cry from healing, and in this situation we are only revealing that we have found a new use for our old friend, the anti-motivator called shame. When entrenched perfectionism reaches this point, we can become tragically out of sync with our own identity.

YOURS,

Tad

Letter Nine: The Crisis of Identity in the Perfectionist

DEAR BELOVED,

My expectations for my teenage self were completely unrealistic. The failure to meet those ridiculously high expectations seriously diminished my ability to love and accept myself. I was so focused on training and racing as a cyclist during my first two years of high school that I didn't spend much time with friends and was largely disconnected from social life. Adolescence is a crucial time in the life of every person. It's the time when our personal identity is solidified and we learn how to relate to ourselves and others as young adults. Since my interests were different from those of others my age, I felt out of place. I searched for my identity in my own imagination, mostly while alone on my bicycle. I would imagine all the races I would win and the places I would go, and pretend to be Eddy Merckx or Greg Lemond, great cycling legends of the twentieth century. The end of a rancher's fence might serve as my finish line, so I could sprint toward it and then throw my hands up in victory.

The hills south of town were my Pyrenees Mountains, and I imagined myself winning a mountaintop stage in the Tour de France. At home I would watch the races I had recorded on VHS tapes and read any book I could find on cycling. In some ways it was easier to live in my imagination (where everything could be perfect, and perfectly controlled) than to deal with the things a normal teenager confronts at 15-16 years old.

The realization of our true self is not usually accomplished during childhood, but the path to such a realization is often stunted there. As we grow from childhood to adulthood the ego self, which serves its purpose of protecting and propelling the child through the confusing changes of adolescence, must diminish and make room for a more expansive self. One which seeks for meaning, values the humility of service, and attempts to transcend the emptiness and suffering which manifest in our lives from time to time. It's the true self, not the ego self, which is capable of spiritual connection with others. The realization of the true self is critical to a person's healthy sense of belonging (there is such a thing as a distorted sense of belonging). A true community is a grouping of true selves, a collection of people free to be authentic and vulnerable.

A crisis of identity happens in the perfectionist when the true self is not realized, and the ego self remains empowered to search for a superficial covering. This is one of the side effects of the refusal to love and accept oneself in a state of perceived imperfection. Simply put, the running after an identity which is acceptable to me prevents me from ever knowing my true self. That true self is relegated to a place on the sidelines while the perfectionist runs after illusions.

It would have been harmless if my role-playing were limited to these games on the bicycle which played out on the roads of West Texas. Unfortunately for me, there was something more profound at work, and it would continue deep into my adult life. As I followed the arc of perfectionism to the end, my life became one long identity crisis made up of hundreds of smaller ones. When you don't love and accept yourself the way you are, or make peace with the reality around you, you try to become someone else. Someone that people love and adore. Someone you might be able to live with.

At some point early in my life I formed the habit of putting on different personas in hopes that I would find a "back door" into peace and self-acceptance. I didn't. Most of the people around me thought I was different and unique, because I didn't follow the crowd. It's true, I didn't want to be like everyone else. I did however secretly want to be *someone* else. Usually I chose someone specific, someone accomplished whom people seemed to admire, and tried to emulate many of their strengths, habits, and mannerisms. Since I didn't reveal this deep, dark secret of my confused identity to anyone (I was too ashamed–there's that shame and fear again), people rarely noticed that I was mimicking someone else. Sometimes they did notice, and I eventually opened up about it after I burned out. Once I recognized and confronted this aspect of perfectionism, I never felt any desire to repeat this behavior again. I may not be *thrilled* with who I am every day, but I'm committed to being and loving myself.

If you haven't followed the arc of perfectionism very far, this might not be a problem for you. But I wanted to tell you about it so you can be on guard for this sneaky symptom of perfectionism which is rarely talked about. It comes on slowly and might seem like child's play at first, but when it continues for years or even decades it can cause incredible pain.

Let's agree on one thing. It's the perfectionism telling us that we don't have something special to offer to the world. It's the distortion of the perfectionist filter I wrote about in a previous letter that leads us to *believe* that we don't. And it's the voice of the accuser which tells us every day not to put our own creativity out into the world. It not only prevents us from living our truth, it prevents us from ever finding our truth by experience. Why does perfectionism, that refusal to love and accept ourselves in a state of imperfection, keep us from really experiencing fully *our own* abundant life, taking it in and processing it in a way that allows wisdom and confident creativity to flourish? The answer is to be found in our need for security and the strategy we use to meet this need.

YOURS,

Tad

Letter Ten: The Need for Security and the Strategy of Control

DEAR BELOVED,

Sadly, no one ever spoke to me about the relationship between needs, feelings, and strategies. Not until I was over 40 years old, that is. By that time I had listened to and considered the spiritual problems of hundreds of people in my capacity as an Orthodox Christian priest. Sometimes it was just a quick confession that got my mind turning, and sometimes it was an ongoing relationship with a person who was trying to find a path to more joy, peace, and harmony in life with God's help. I had not expected to delve so deeply into the spiritual problems of other people when I entered the monastery. Not every monk serves as a priest, and there are monks who hardly converse with other people at all. I was asked to serve as a priest about three years after my arrival at the monastery because most of the resident priests were elderly and not able to keep up with the demands of the daily liturgical services. Without really planning to, I had become a student of people. I often felt like a piece of the puzzle was missing in my understanding of how people related to themselves, each other, and even to their image of God. Why so much conflict? When I learned about the simple but profound teaching of Marshall B. Rosenberg, I knew it was the missing part. Rosenberg taught a system of empathic connection with our own needs and feelings, and those of others. He called the system Nonviolent Communication, and it's a system which has been used around the world to resolve everyday conflicts on a small scale (between two people) and bloody conflicts on a large scale (between warring ethnic groups). In this system, empathy is the goal, and empathy is defined as a connection which is borne of a deep understanding and acceptance of the needs and feelings of both parties in the conflict. This requires a commitment to the practice of listening without evaluation until the empathic connection is established. It turns out that this system is not only useful for conflicts between as few as two people, it's also the path to real self-knowledge.

After all, the most spiritual person in the world has to begin by becoming human. We can't skip that step.

Since people are rarely taught this all-encompassing system of communication when they are young, most of us live our lives in a sort of unconscious frenzy, reacting to the forms of communication we receive, and communicating to others without an awareness of what is at the heart of our conflicts and misunderstandings. If we step back for a moment and ask the questions, "what need is she trying to meet with the way she is communicating to me" and "what needs am I trying to meet with my words and behavior," we begin to see that we all have something in common. We all have needs we would like met.

The needs of others might not make sense to us, and our needs might not make sense to them. But if we want the power of *empathic connection* in our lives, we will need to recognize and respect the needs and feelings of others.

When it comes to *empathic connection* with the self, the perfectionist can often display a baffling combination of two states which may seem contradictory. The perfectionist is *self-centered* in that he wants the world to bend and bow to his standards and expectations, but is terribly disconnected from his authentic self. Why is this? The answer lies in the lack of self-empathy with which the perfectionist carries on his daily life. He's running frantically after an ideal, and never stops to "get in touch" with himself to find out what needs are driving his behaviors, and what feelings are coming up in the midst of his pursuit of perfection. Anyone in such a state is bound to experience conflict, both with himself and others.

The ways in which we try to meet our needs (whether we are conscious of them or not) are called *strategies*. And it's the strategies that can really get us into trouble. The strategies aren't evil. It's just that when we use them unconsciously they can lead us into dark and confusing places.

When it comes to perfectionism there are many needs we could speak about, but the one that seems to overshadow all others is the need for security. We feel afraid, because all around us we see threats to our pursuit of perfection. For the anorexic perfectionist it might be Thanksgiving dinner. For the athletic perfectionist it might be a sickness that causes a missed day of training. If I allow perfectionism to take over my whole life, I will hardly be able to sleep, having finished the day with so many things left un-perfected. I'll be too anxious to attack the un-perfected first thing the next morning. You see, what we really want is a promise that we are moving toward perfection, always walking forward and never backward, and on track to arrive at our destination (where the love and acceptance we are withholding lay waiting) as quickly as possible. In other words, we need security.

I can prove this to you with one simple word which is familiar to every perfectionist: control. Control is the strategy we employ to meet our need for security. And it can make us do some pretty crazy things. Getting ourselves and everything around us under control is job #1 every day for the hardened perfectionist. The more we can control, the more we feel assured of our eventual arrival at that highest of goals, perfection.

I would like to point out one strange paradox that I have found to be universally true. The controller is also easily controlled. That is, examine closely any great controller (a powerful person who seems to exert total control in his or her own sphere) and you will find hidden behind the curtain another force, person, or substance which controls the controller. This paradox becomes less surprising when we apply what we now know about the strategy of control. It is borne of an insatiable need for security, and it's driven by fear and shame. This means that the seemingly invincible controller has buttons to push just like everyone else. No one is exempt from the natural law of needs, feelings, and strategies.

Now, it sometimes happens that perfectionists hit a "sweet-spot" in life. This happens when everything lines up and gives them a chance to control a capable group of people under their authority and accomplish great things quickly. That's when they feel as if they have boundless energy and don't feel the need to connect with themselves at all. All the action is on the outside and humming along like clockwork. But human nature is frail, and when serious obstacles eventually arise, the perfectionist finds himself shattered and confused. Not being in touch with ourselves (our needs, feelings and strategies) carries a high price.

If we look at the foundation of all basic human needs, I think we could agree that everyone really just wants to be loved. It's only natural that we try to meet our need for love—the love we often refuse ourselves—not only through relationships with other human beings but with a higher power much greater than us. In the next letter we will look at how we bring our spiritual problem of perfectionism into the realm of our spiritual and religious pursuits.

YOURS,

Tad

Letter Eleven: Spiritual Perfectionism

DEAR BELOVED,

One of the peculiarities of my childhood was an intense interest in spiritual things. I had an acute sense of wonder, and it seemed to me that the spiritual world was very close by, only separated from the visible world by a thin veil–one that was often pierced. I sensed and experienced the presence of God in both nature and temples. I have been trying to understand and write about the experiences of my childhood—like that epiphany on a warm Spring day in the Rocky Mountains at the age of ten—all my life. I understand that everyone's spiritual history is unique, and I don't know the details of yours. What's interesting to me as I write to you now is how my perfectionism —my refusal to love and accept myself in a state of imperfection —informed my spiritual life as I grew and evolved.

As a teenager I only experienced a great need for security in certain aspects of my life, and in other areas I felt more free- dom. I loved to read spiritual books from a wide range of traditions, find common themes, and in general revel in the mystery of God which seemed to me to be boundless and infinite. My faith in practice however was simple. It was enough for me to be aware of my personal relationship with God, and I never felt restricted in my exploration of what other people in different cultures believed or practiced in their own pursuit of the Divine. The spiritual life was a world of possibilities, and everywhere I looked I saw the fingerprints of God as he made himself known throughout history.

In my 20's something began to change. Perfectionism was becoming more of a problem in my life. The signs and symptoms were everywhere. I was growing more anxious, more obsessive, and more confused about my identity and calling with each passing year. When my relationships began to suffer —because I was so hard on myself and equally hard on others— my need for security was activated in an enormous way. It never occurred to me to get help from a therapist. My solution was to stop trying to improve my relationships with other people and get control of my relationship with God. I became obsessed with dogma, ritual, and correctness in my spiritual life. Simply put, I needed to find the perfect system for getting as close to God as quickly as possible. I wanted the perfect training program, but this time it wasn't for a sport. It was for the spiritual life. Only 18 months from the time of my initial discovery of what I believed to be the perfect system and the answer to my need for spiritual security, I had already entered a monastery where I would remain for 16 years. Yes, I had committed my life to God (for the third or fourth time) but I had also unknowingly signed a contract with perfectionism. The promise of perfectionism in the contract turned out to be false (I didn't become perfect) and it took me 16 years to realize that as beautiful and wonderful as the monastic life is, I had built my spiritual life on entirely the wrong foundation–the pernicious pride of perfectionism.

I don't mean to say I have regrets. Actually, this entire process was required so that I could learn about perfectionism. Otherwise I would not be able to write these letters to you today. I'm grateful for everything I experienced.

I was very naive, completely trusting and had a sort of "babe lost in the woods" personality even at the age of 25. Besides the fact that I was fulfilling my need for security, lurking under the surface were two destructive aspects of my self. One, I needed to punish myself for all my failures. Two, though I had been taught about the unconditional love of God from my childhood and had spoken of this love to others, I had somehow developed an entirely different image of God. The way I behaved, the way I prayed, and even my world view revealed what I really believed–that I must become perfect in order to earn God's love. And if I believed that about God, what right did I have to love and accept myself in such a state of imperfection?

The bottom line is, some people start out with a sincere intention to serve God, or transform themselves spiritually, and get derailed along the way. I know, because it happened to me. When I saw myself becoming the opposite of what I envisioned, I needed to understand why. Hadn't I left the world and entered a monastery to serve God, be transformed by the profound ascetical and mystical traditions of Eastern Orthodox Christianity? Hadn't I read hundreds of spiritual books, served hundreds of liturgies and kept the fasts prescribed by the

Church? I knew I had met holy people, some of the best examples of personal transformation in my chosen tradition. Externally, I had the visible marks of my devotion–the long hair and beard (according to the Orthodox Christian tradition), the cross around my neck, and the black robes of a monk. I also know that I helped a lot of people, because they tell me so to this day. Why did I become so out of harmony with my daily life? Why did I become so stressed-out, irritable, anxious and depressed? The answer is, I didn't know myself. My untreated (and therefore unhealed) perfectionism blocked the way to true self-knowledge, and my lack of boundaries and self-care allowed toxic relationships to drain my energy completely.

I wasn't the first person to miss out on the transformation which spiritual practice offers due to a preoccupation with externals, and I won't be the last. The psychotherapist and author John Welwood calls this phenomenon "spiritual bypassing." In his counseling work with people who had spent decades in devout spiritual practice he noticed that many bypass the hard and often painful work of spiritual transformation and instead focus their attention on the trappings of religion. It's especially easy to do this when the externals of a religion are exotic, and the rituals complex. The point is, you can shave your head or grow your beard and hair long, and put on black robes or colorful ones. You can be elevated within the hierarchy of your religious order, and even get closer to the elder, master, or teacher–and still miss the inner transformation. For some it is simply a matter of missing the spiritual message and getting busy with the boards, committees, and finances that are a part of the earthly life of any religious institution. The politics of any institution can easily obscure the purpose for which the institution was created if the communication between members becomes violent.

Perfectionists are especially prone to this kind of derailment. There is a tremendous amount of pain associated with the guilt, shame, and penchant for self-punishment that drives perfectionists. It's easier to focus on the externals (and what others are doing or not doing) than to go deep inside and begin the hard work of authentic transformation. This transformation can only begin with self-knowledge. Build your spiritual structure on any other foundation, and you are sure to be building it on sand. Real spirituality is impossible until we truly meet ourselves.

The last thing the ego wants is to take a trip into the depths of the human heart where we meet all of our pain and trauma, unmet needs and violent emotions. Any distraction will suffice, even a religious one.

No matter how deep or complex, how rigid or flexible, how beautiful or mystical any religion is, it cannot be properly called a religion unless there are people practicing it. Religion as revelation may spring forth from the heavenly or unseen realms, but it cannot escape its anthropological roots. However uniform the dogma, we cannot escape the fact that each person who hears the words and experiences the rituals brings something unique into the atmosphere created by the structure. Each person brings with him the sum total of his genes, his experiences, his conscious and subconscious mind. In other words, each brings an entire *world* with him. When this personal world collides with the world of the religious group, the results can be hard to predict.

Sometimes we are forced into the process of personal transformation through the exhaustion of our natural forces. This exhaustion is called *burnout*. When it happens, the perfectionist must choose between life or death. And life can only be met on its own terms.

YOURS,

Tad

Letter Twelve: Burnout and the Darkness of Transformation

DEAR BELOVED,

The real question is, how long can a person go on living in a state of refusal–refusal to love and accept himself for the simple fact of his imperfection. It's like asking how long a person can hold his breath underwater. It depends on the person, and how much they flail and use up the air in their lungs. Love is the oxygen which fuels life. Without love life takes on a gloomy aspect. Perfectionism leads to burnout.

Burnout is a result of total spiritual, mental, and physical exhaustion. It is usually a sign that we are not in harmony with the circumstances of our life–perhaps even that we are in a state of war with our own life. It is a form of trauma, and its effects can be far-reaching.

What does burnout look like? It's a sudden darkness that comes on when our energy is entirely spent. When it happens, a person suddenly finds that his old strategies don't work anymore. It's no longer possible to exert control and keep the much-feared chaos at bay. Neither is it possible to ignore our human needs and feelings. When burnout happens to us, nothing makes sense and we realize that we have to learn an entirely new way of living. When it happens after a long period of stress and becomes a form of trauma, it can actually affect the workings of the brain. After a burnout, a person who once attacked the affairs of the day with vigor suddenly finds he can't even mentally process basic information.

This is what happened to me. Any external stimulus, such as a request for a decision about some important matter, initiated a strange sensation. I could feel a burning sensation up the back of my neck which settled into my head. And I heard nothing. I felt helpless and frightened, and wondered if my brain would ever function normally again.

For the perfectionist, burnout is "hitting bottom." It's much like the bottom which finally convinces an alcoholic to enter treatment or begin the twelve steps. The first of those twelve steps is to admit our powerlessness in the face of the problem.

Burnout is not the end. It's a new beginning.

Naturally, people prefer quick fixes and easy solutions. Real transformation takes time and work. There is one theme which is found in all spiritual traditions. It's also right in front of us, embedded in the natural world and the cycle of the seasons. It's the theme of Death and Resurrection, Winter and Spring. In order to experience real transformation, we have to "die" and experience a powerful darkness. Only then can we rise to live again, renewed and transformed. A burnout is a sort of death. At times the darkness may seem overwhelming. But beautiful gifts often come in ugly boxes. If a perfectionist doesn't act to counter the spiritual illness on his own while the symptoms are mild, the beautiful gift of an invitation to transformation will eventually come. When it arrives, it's to be found inside the ugly box of burnout, which brings everything to a halt and forces the recipient of the invitation to choose between life and death.

In the coming letters I will show you why the pain of perfectionism is a beautiful gift in an ugly box, and how the lessons it teaches us open up a whole new world of self-knowledge, freedom, and love. In order to access those lessons we first need to look inside and begin practicing the art of observation.

YOURS,

Tad

Letter Thirteen: The Beginning of Observation

DEAR BELOVED,

Where do we begin our journey from perfectionism—our refusal to love and accept ourselves in a state of imperfection— to an abundant life filled inside and out with love? We begin with observation.

All of our running and reacting, controlling and cursing has led us to become strangers to ourselves and the present moment. In short, perfectionism leads to a state of spiritual *disconnection*.

If we have truly grown tired of the fruits of our spiritual disconnection, it's time to begin a practice of observation which can be done anywhere we find ourselves. It's quite simple really. We just need to observe. Every day we experience many stimuli. The stimuli and our reactions to them have always been there, but we probably didn't observe either very well in our state of disconnection.

Is there someone in your life who knows how to push the

buttons of shame or fear in order to motivate you (or keep you from moving)? How does this process work? What kind of verbal and nonverbal communication do they employ to push this button? What are the thoughts and emotions which begin to move inside you? If you react defensively, what happens then? If you respond to the guilt-trip by giving them what they seek, do you find yourself doing something you are not in harmony with? If you were more aware of this process, might you choose another way, one in which you acknowledge their need but then communicate honestly and without violence your reason for not acting upon the stimulus of the guilt-trip?

What are the words you use in self-talk? Words have power. What do you feel when you use one word or another in your self-talk? What kind of results are you seeking by using those words? Do the words lead to the desired result?

If it helps you to write down your observations, keep a journal as a record of your newfound awareness once or twice a day.

Now comes the difficult part. We must assume total responsibility for our thoughts and emotions, our spiritual illnesses, and all of our actions. Blaming others and thinking of ourselves as victims will not help us to reach our goal. Breaking free from perfectionism is like starting a non-violent revolution. All must be pardoned, and everyone must be forgiven—including ourselves. From this day forward we hold to this principle: "No one can hurt me unless I first give them permission."

What we *want* is a different experience of life. For this we need knowledge. Self-knowledge to be exact. Observation is the art of gathering the information we need from ourselves. If we process the information wisely, we will arrive at self-knowledge. A happy byproduct of this observation is a new state of deeper connection with ourselves.

Observation is so important that we must continue the practice for our entire life, especially when we notice we are losing the empathic connection with ourselves. As you will see, this cornerstone of our new way of being opens the door to self-compassion.

YOURS,

Tad

Letter Fourteen: The Language of Love and Self-compassion

DEAR BELOVED,

The English language doesn't do a very good job with love. Perhaps this is why self-love is such a confusing topic for some people. Languages like Sanskrit and ancient Persian use dozens of words to describe the various forms of love. The Greeks employed six different terms to describe different types of love. Although there is only one Greek word, *philautia,* which describes the love of self, the pre-Christian Greek philosophers separated this definition in two. We should follow suit, and make the distinction between narcissistic self-love and healthy self-love. The distinction is critical, because the healthy form of *philautia* gives us the freedom to turn our love outward and share it with others, while narcissistic self-love is destructive. Let's call the healthy form of *philautia* self-compassion.

We perfectionists (especially spiritual or moral perfectionists) shudder at the thought that we might be less than perfect at loving others. While lacking self-compassion, we might also fear being exposed as selfish narcissists. But selfishness is one thing, and self-compassion is another thing altogether. It's time for a reality check. In allowing perfectionism to run our life through our *lack* of self-compassion, we have become the selfishness we so despised. The result of our perfectionism is an insidious preoccupation with ourselves. We are caught in a conundrum and fail to live up to our lofty theoretical standard of selfless love for others. Then we feel ashamed and...well, this is the whole story of our life isn't it? How do we escape this cycle and learn to truly love ourselves *and* others?

Being self-centered never made anyone happy. Selfless love (*agape* in the Greek language of love) on the other hand, has the power to raise us "from earth to heaven." The problem for perfectionists is, simply put–you can't get there from here. What I mean is, there's more than one step from being a neurotic bundle of obsessive-compulsive thoughts at war with myself and the world around me to *becoming love*. We first need to become *free* to love. The path to this freedom runs through self-compassion.

What's the most loving thing you can do for another person? There are many possible answers, but I am not alone in asserting that the most loving thing you can do for another person is to be present with them. Being totally present for another person doesn't require money, an academic degree, a license, or even words. You aren't even required to speak their language. There's something magical about total presence, and by that I mean it is deeply spiritual and hard to quantify. It does require non-judgement and empathic connection. It can take the form of listening, but it is more than that. Real presence makes the space for love. It is love in action, even if to the outside observer very little seems to be "going on." If we want to acquire the gift of being present, we must begin by being present with ourselves. See how self-compassion suddenly becomes a prerequisite for a love turned outward?

As I wrote previously, allowing perfectionism to go unchecked for long periods in our life can lead to a state of profound disconnection with ourselves, other people, and the world around us. We are disconnected from the present moment because we are planning our assault on the future. We are disconnected from ourselves because it's too painful to look at that abandoned child suffering inside us, and we turn away in disgust. We are disconnected from others because, as we pursued our strategy of control, we stopped seeing them as unique expressions of the Divine image and developed a tendency to ask ourselves only one question about them: *How do they fit in to our pursuit of perfection?*

Is it painful to read this? If you feel something stirring in your heart as you connect with this pain, then you have just made the first step toward self-compassion, though you probably didn't realize it. This is where we take the practice of observation to the next level. The only way to begin the work of self-compassion is to go inside and acknowledge the pain. We can also acknowledge the fear of touching that pain. Go to that place where the pain resides. What do you notice? Ignore the voices which accuse you and tell you stories about what the pain says about you, the voices which proclaim judgment saying "the fact that you are depressed means you are bad–just give up." They aren't helpful. Self-empathy only arises in an environment of non-judgement. You've spent enough time proclaiming judgements on yourself already. Again, what do you notice? Fear? Get in touch with the fear, and send love there. Beyond the fear you may find more pain. Get in touch with the pain, and send love to that place. Once you have done even this, already you have become less disconnected from yourself than you were a short time before.

Here is something we perfectionists don't like to hear: We can only begin from the place where we find ourselves now. We'd rather pretend that with a few quick actions we can put our interior life in order. But since it's much easier to clean the entire house, wash the car, go shopping and stock the pantry—in other words put everything around us in perfect order—we never really get around to ordering our spiritual lives. We might even do "spiritual things" or "churchy things" in order to avoid the real spiritual work of meeting ourselves in that place where the pain resides.

There are people who object to self-compassion, fearing that it will lead them to a state of self-pity and inaction. This is a great misunderstanding. Self-pity has nothing to do with self-compassion. When we relate to ourselves in a compassionate way, we are moving past unproductive pity and using the motivating force of love to heal our wounds as quickly as possible so that we can continue to be of service to Life. Self-pity is a dark room and a giant bowl of ice cream that leads to a state of paralysis. Self-compassion is an invigorating swim in a healing spring that puts us back on track to add value to our life and the lives of those around us.

Others object to self-compassion because they believe it leads to selfishness. But selfishness is really the preoccupation with the perfection of the self, which is the albatross of perfectionists.

The purpose of self-compassion is a movement beyond this preoccupation. The goal is to emerge whole and healthy, free and unburdened by the weight of shame and fear. Self-compassion empowers us to make the world a more loving place, one heart at a time.

The literal definition of compassion is "suffering with." Compassion can't exist without the presence of suffering. The question is, what kind of suffering do we want in our life? As children, we probably tried to avoid pain by putting up defenses. This led to the profound disconnection which causes us suffering now. We can choose to continue suffering the pain of disconnection (and hold on tightly to our perfectionism) or choose the path to freedom which passes through a different kind of suffering. Self-compassion begins with pain, but it leads to peace, joy, and an abundance of love. Once we taste this love and recognize it as the force which gives life meaning, we can turn and offer it to others. We can't give something we don't have.

YOURS,

Tad

Letter Fifteen: Learning to Laugh at Ourselves

DEAR BELOVED,

Today something happened which reminded me of something very important I've been wanting to write about. Once we settle down enough to admit that we have a problem with perfectionism, one of the best things we can do is to laugh at ourselves. Perfectionism is often not very funny, because it causes so many serious problems in our life. But there is humor in it, and finding that humor is part of the healing process.

This morning, as almost every morning, I wanted to write. Then I realized I was doing *that thing* again. That obsessive, compulsive, controlling thing. I started a cup of coffee in the espresso machine, then I went to look for some paper I could use to mind-map a future book. I found some at the nearby desk, and then went to look for marking pens in a range of colors. I found some, but I got hung up on the fact that the red was an extra fine point marking pen, and the others were the usual fine point markers. I couldn't bear the thought of the mind-map looking any less than perfect, so I dug around in the desk until I found a red one that matched the thickness of the others. What a relief! Can you imagine what would have happened if I had not found the perfect red sharpie? Yes, I know it's ridiculous. The coffee was sitting there this whole time, and if you have used an espresso machine you know that it comes out at just the right temperature, and since it is only really less than one-half of a cup of coffee, it cools quickly. Even though I knew this, I still didn't drop everything and enjoy the coffee. I noticed that the water reservoir was half-empty, and the used-cartridge receptacle was almost full. This bothered me, so I put the cup of coffee aside, filled the reservoir, emptied the receptacle and put everything back together. Finally, I sat down to enjoy the coffee. It was cold. And honestly, if I had noticed that the trash was full (okay, more than three-quarters full) that would have bothered me, and I would have taken the trash outside and replaced the bag as well before enjoying my coffee, which would have been even colder by that time. I did resist the impulse to organize everything on the kitchen counter and wash dishes before sitting down with the coffee. And it's a good thing there wasn't any laundry in process, or I would have had to make that whole laundry situation perfect as well.

This is all very petty, I know. I'm not comparing my problem of an arduous journey to a cold cup of coffee with the immense suffering in the world. But this little story, in which no one was injured or harmed in any way, is just a small example of what's left of my perfectionistic habits.

This episode reminded me of how I used to behave. Whenever I cooked for myself, I couldn't enjoy the meal until I had already cleaned up all the pots and pans and put all the ingredients away. I ate a lot of cold meals. I used to put virtually everything in plastic bags before I put them in suitcases when packing for a trip. You should have seen my sock drawer. It was immaculate.

There was also a time when the daily manifestations of my perfectionism were much more serious. I started the day on high alert, looking for any sign of disorder in my surroundings or in the monks under my authority, and breathlessly attacked it all in order to put things "right." If someone pointed out to me that I was being far too intense, or accused me of having obsessive-compulsive disorder, I was offended. Me, disorder? Actually, I think the more the disorder increased on the inside, the more I tried to put right the disorder on the outside.

This morning I had a good laugh with my friend about my arduous journey toward a cold cup of coffee. I'm glad I can laugh at myself, and glad that my neurotic behavior these days is usually not much more serious than this example.

You've suffered a lot from your perfectionism, but you're on the right track and everything will be okay. Find a reason to laugh at yourself today. Or go out and play like a child again. It will do your heart some good. As the saying goes: *Why walk when you can dance?*

YOURS,

Tad

Letter Sixteen: Authenticity, Vulnerability, and Belonging

DEAR BELOVED,

Learning to laugh at ourselves is one step in the right direction if our goal is to be authentic and vulnerable. It's one sign that we've made a decision to put down our shield and stop pretending to have everything under control.

What does it mean to be authentic? It means to rejoice more in questions than answers. It turns out that we all have the same questions about what it means to be human. Connection means sharing our individual experiences as we explore these questions with mutual empathy and presence. The moment one of us substitutes evaluation for presence, authenticity is threatened. Judgement is like the water which quickly puts out the fire of authenticity.

Sometimes it seems that everything is working against our struggle for authenticity. The world around us is constantly sending messages about how we *should* be (or look or act or feel). This is a particular problem for perfectionists who have spent years disconnected from any tangible sense of an authentic self. The stimulus of the world around me often encourages a continuation of the identity crisis which made authenticity impossible in the first place.

We must understand that authenticity is not only a necessary component of the new way of being we aspire to, but a barometer which offers us an honest assessment of our rejection of perfectionism. Authenticity is worth fighting for. How do we acquire it and integrate it within ourselves? In my experience there are four key actions we must take:

- Start with one person.
- Master the art of observation.
- Write a letter to that abandoned child within.
- When necessary, use a sword.

Allow me to expand on each of these actions...

CHOOSE ONE PERSON who really believes in you, and tell them about your struggle with perfectionism and how important authenticity is to you now. This might be someone close to you who has suffered from the outward manifestations of your perfectionism. You probably have a sense of how you have hurt that person, *and* a sense that despite all that, they have a capacity for unconditional love. Now is the time to be vulnerable with that person, to stop putting on airs and pretending to be perfect. This act of vulnerability is guaranteed to be rewarding. If your hunch is right (and it probably is), this person will support you and rejoice with you as you set out on this new journey and experience this new way of being. Beginning the journey toward authenticity with one trusted person increases our level of confidence so that we can then open up in a vulnerable way with a second and a third...and eventually make this a way of life.

UNLESS WE BECOME HERMITS, we will never be able to avoid the stimulus which threatens authenticity. Actually, you would be surprised how forcefully present this stimulus is even for hermits. I can attest that it takes many years for a monk to forget all the messaging his mind and heart tucked away during his pre-monastic life. Whatever our external circumstances, we can choose to live in one of two ways. We can set ourselves up like a mindless receiver of information and let all the garbage just wash over us while we stand wide-eyed and helpless. Or we can master the art of observation. Forming the habit of continual self-empathy is the key to processing the information that comes to us in a way that makes us more wise and discerning. At first we may need some time to process a given stimulus. The world can wait. Jumping to answer an email or respond to a perceived insult prevents us from getting in touch with our needs and feelings, working with our thoughts and emotions, and learning all we can from every experience. In future letters we will explore the ways in which we can take observation to another level and begin to purify the heart.

AUTHENTICITY AND VULNERABILITY come naturally for children. There are exceptions of course, and for some childhood is cut short by trauma. Even with the exceptions, the principle is still universal. It's the reason Jesus said that we must become like children in order to enter the heavenly kingdom. The moment I scolded my child within, sent him into the corner and abandoned him in my drive for perfection was the moment my authenticity and vulnerability were compromised. From that moment, these two qualities became frightening for me. I need that child now. I need to make peace with him, express my unconditional love for him and make a request: please forgive me and return to me the authenticity and vulnerability I under-valued, but now need so desperately.

Authenticity and vulnerability are the two halves that make the whole of a "sense of wonder" possible. The presence of these two qualities is a sign that we are emerging from the isolation of perfectionism. The result is a renewed sense of awe at the beauty and interconnectedness of everything and everyone. I can no longer live without the sense of wonder only he (the child) can help me to recover. It's time to write that child a letter, and invite him to walk through life with me again. There is plenty of evidence across spiritual traditions and human history that authenticity and vulnerability are prerequisites for a profound experience of God. We perfectionists often imagine the opposite. We think that our experience of God will come after we "get it all together." We hear the voice of The Beloved calling us into a relationship and respond by saying "come back later, when I have everything in order." Children aren't hindered by this kind of complex thinking, which is why the spiritual world is so accessible to them.

FINALLY, there are times when we have to use a sword. Much of our decision to reject perfectionism and our journey toward a new way of being involves becoming softer, more flexible, and more vulnerable. But we have to know when it is time for an act which, though seemingly violent, is really in the best interest of ourselves and others. It happened in my life that I became emotionally connected with a couple of people whom I permitted to motivate me—through shame and fear—to think, feel, and react in ways that were destructive for me. Standing up to those people and cutting off their influence in my life were important steps on the path to inner freedom. However intense the interaction when we pull out our sword and use it, we must cultivate empathy and love in the midst of the act, and after the separation. However big, important, and threatening the other seems to us, they are still humans like us with their own needs, feelings and strategies. It's entirely possible to make a drastic change in our association and even end a relationship in a spirit of love, empathy, and forgiveness. What's required is the humility to admit that we played our own part in the story of this relationship. You might even say we *created it* because our own needs and strategies were at work during the formation of the relationship.

WE ALL WANT TO *BELONG*. We have a need for a sense of belonging. The problem is that we go about meeting this need in an unconscious way, offering to become whatever the group we want to belong to wants us to be. It requires faith to reverse our strategy for meeting this need, and begin with being authentic. Having the faith to believe we will attract and find the people we really *belong with* is an important part of the struggle for authenticity. Now we are approaching a more concrete question. What does a new way of being really look like?

YOURS,

Tad

Letter Seventeen: What a New Way of Being Really Looks Like

DEAR BELOVED,

Every area of our lives will be touched by our rejection of perfectionism, the decision to love and accept ourselves, and the development of a new way of being. What does a new way of being really look like in practice?

As perfectionists we fear loosening our grip on life. To understand why, all we have to do is look back at the definition we began with: **perfectionism is the refusal to love and accept oneself in a state of imperfection.** It's no wonder we "white knuckle" our way down the road of life. Our most intimate, sacred, and unavoidable relationship is at stake–our relationship with ourselves. The possibility of living our entire life in a state of self-hatred if we don't "get this right" hangs over our head like an executioner's sword.

We must now commit ourselves to a new way of being. It's like changing the fuel we run our engine on. Instead of running on a fuel that gets us down the road but corrodes our engine and eventually breaks it, we need to run our engine on something which provides infinite energy while continuously renewing the engine itself. And that "miracle fuel" is love. Love is made up of many components. If we want a stable and reliable love to fuel our engine and accompany us in every situation, we need all the components: connection, empathy, presence, compassion, boundaries, honesty, authenticity, vulnerability, gratitude, and intuition. Mindfully keeping all these components intact as we encounter pressures of various kinds is a skill we must learn as we commit ourselves to this new way of being.

The impacts of this new way of being will be witnessed first in two places: how we approach goals and accomplishments, and how we relate to the people who became a part of our story as we lived out our perfectionism. So let's talk about goals and relationships.

Breaking up with perfectionism doesn't mean giving up all of our hopes and dreams and sitting around feeling sorry for ourselves. We can still achieve our goals, live boldly, be ambitious, and make an impact on the world. Recent research in neuroscience and behavior has shown that self-compassion actually increases motivation and success. My decision to reject perfectionism is a decision to love and accept myself now, no matter how imperfect I am. I have very ambitious goals for the next seven months. But for the first time in my life I'm setting those goals consciously, and being honest with myself. And I'm doing it all from a place of self-compassion. My motivation is no longer guilt or fear or shame, but love. I want to be the best person I can be for myself and others. Even if this was always my desire, the change is in the motivation.

Write down your goals. Then wait a bit and check them with fresh eyes, and ask yourself if they are realistic. Of course, we can never be 100 percent sure about what is realistic, but we can ask questions like "what if I get one flu and one cold this year, and other normal 'life events' happen such as a wedding, a funeral, and a spontaneous trip to the beach–will I still be able to realistically accomplish these goals while making space for life?" We want to be available for life. We want to say yes to life and to the surprises which life has in store for us. Revise your goals and timelines to make the space for life.

Then comes the important part. Look at your goals and set the tone with statements like these:

- Today I am beginning the necessary work to achieve these goals from a place of self-love.
- Whether I achieve all of these goals or come up short, I will still love myself.
- When I see the faults in myself that hold me back from accomplishing these goals, I will empathically heal those weaknesses with love and forgiveness.
- I am totally responsible for all that happens in my life. No one can hurt me–that's my job alone.

Since as perfectionists we have a history of connecting our level of accomplishment with our estimation of self-worth, we must approach this area of our life consciously. How we handle ourselves as we interact with our goals and accomplishments is the first real litmus test. It's a test which will reveal our commitment to a new way of being.

When it comes to relationships, one of the difficult things about recovering from perfectionism is the question of who to listen to. On one hand, perfectionism became a problem for us as a result of our stubbornness. We blocked out the loving voices in our lives which pleaded with us not to be so hard on ourselves, the voices which tried to soothe us with perspective. On the other hand, as our perfectionism became more entrenched, we began to enter into unhealthy relationships. That is, people with needs to meet noticed that they could get what they wanted from us if they applied the right kinds of pressure. It's as if we displayed two buttons for all to see, one on each shoulder. One was the shame button, and the other was the fear button. Taking full responsibility for our lives means removing these buttons. Sometimes more work is required (including therapy) to find and heal the sources of the shame and fear which have affected so many of our relationships.

We don't want to stubbornly block out the voice of every person in our life, but we need to be discerning when other people give us advice or try to steer us one way or another in our vulnerable state. If we don't learn new tools for communication, we can both miss out on helpful words from others *and* fall back into unhealthy relationships constructed on a foundation of shame and fear. If we are really committed to a new way of being, we need the help of intuition. Perfectionism silences the voice of intuition by keeping us disconnected from ourselves. But intuition can be recovered quickly if we have the courage to go where it resides. In order to find it we need to visit a new place where both painful memories and tremendous power are located. This place is the heart.

YOURS,

Tad

Letter Eighteen: Painful Memories and the Power of the Heart

DEAR BELOVED,

I think of you often and wonder how your journey is unfolding. The decision to do everything from a new place, a place of self-compassion, is not a decision we make only once. It's a decision we make every day. In fact, we make this decision many times each day. In the beginning it can be very difficult. Other people might not understand, because they don't share our history with perfectionism.

I don't know about you, but I really struggled with memories as I began to live this "new way of being." I have memories of the things I did to meet my need for security. I have memories of the toxic relationships I developed on the foundation of my need for love and approval, and the shame of not being *enough*. I also remember my abuse of others, the way I put others down, criticized and dismissed them in hopes of feeling better about myself—holding them up to high expectations they never agreed to. If there is anything which trips me up on this new path of love and acceptance, it's memories. What do we do with them?

First, it's important to realize that memories reside in two places. Naturally, they reside in the mind. They also live in a more mysterious place in the center of our being. There are various ways to describe this center, but we will call it "the heart." There is a lot of evidence that the heart is more than just an organ that pumps blood. It's a second information processing center. It's the place where the emotion of memory lives on long after the inciting incident. And when these emotions are destructive, the heart becomes sick.

Your spiritual practice probably speaks to the treatment of these matters in its own particular way, but I have noticed four universal themes related to purifying the mind and heart of the illness of memories:

- Forgiveness
- Vigilance
- Gratitude
- Love

Forgiving ourselves and others is not always easy, but it's universally rewarding. We never read stories of people who regret their act of forgiveness, but we often read of cycles of revenge that poison the hearts of people and even whole societies when the refusal to forgive is held up as a virtue. Some people refuse to forgive because they think it means forgiveness requires a forgetting and a return to trust. It doesn't work that way. We are free to forgive without returning to a harmful situation. Real forgiveness can take place even if we don't trust ourselves or the other in an unhealthy relationship. Forgiveness is really made up of two components: the act of the will or intellect, and the *release* of the memory in that center of our being, the heart.

In the case of intellect, the decision to forgive might not "stick" the first time. We may need to decide repeatedly to choose the way of forgiveness, and we may need to do something symbolic or meaningful, like write a letter of forgiveness and send it off. If sending it to the person I have in mind is not an option (or if the person I have in mind is myself), I can drop the letter into the ocean or the fire, symbolizing the finality of the act. Let's not forget that we also sometimes need to ask forgiveness of others. The most powerful form of forgiveness is a mutual pardon.

When it comes to the *release* of the memory in the heart, another step is required. For most of us, the mind and the heart are disconnected. Our thoughts run on incessantly, changing the subject and jumping from one thing to another. The heart is then kicked to the curb and left to nurse its wounds. The conscious decision to reconnect the mind and the heart is the single most loving thing we can do for ourselves, and it doesn't require any special equipment or an exotic posture. We simply need to bring the attention of the mind down into the place of the heart and let it dwell there. Some people find it helpful to touch the upper area of the heart or use their breathing to direct the attention of the mind to the place of the heart. Once the attention of the mind is held there where the emotions and illnesses reside, the next step is to replace our usual thoughts with a prayer, or some healing words. If my focus is on forgiveness, I can say "I forgive myself" or "I forgive all and everything" or address ourselves to God asking for forgiveness, mercy, and enlightenment. The union of the mind and the heart is the mechanism whereby our decision to live in the energy of forgiveness becomes a reality at the center of our being. I think of it this way: the mind is the mother who must take the child—the heart—by the hand and gently convince her that the release of the painful memory is in her best interest. In order for this to happen, the mother must drop everything else, visit the child and remain present.

The practice of living with our mind and heart united takes us beyond observation, and toward purification. The cleansing of the painful memories requires the cooperation of the mind and the heart coupled with forgiveness, vigilance, love, and gratitude.

If we have made a decision to live differently and transform the pain of perfectionism into unconditional love and acceptance, we will also need vigilance. The memories of our failures and the wounds we received in the past when we didn't understand the harm perfectionism was doing will return in the form of thoughts and emotions. Vigilance is the immediate recognition of the stimulation we receive when the memories return (the observation we discussed) coupled with our determination to handle them wisely so that we, not the memories, emerge the victor. Vigilance demands an immediate assessment of our needs and feelings upon the arrival of stimulus. Breaking down the components of an otherwise confusing wave of thought and emotion in this way makes me the master of myself instead of a victim of the past. Once I've identified my needs and feelings in any situation, I have a better chance of *acting* in a conscious manner, as opposed to *reacting* without self-awareness.

In the next two letters we will explore the topic of gratitude, and return to the topic of love.

YOURS,

Tad

Letter Nineteen: Gratitude

DEAR BELOVED,

I don't like many of the things I did while I was following the arc of perfectionism. I can't go back to the past and change any of my actions. All I have is the present moment. And in the present moment I can begin with gratitude.

Gratitude is difficult for a perfectionist. If I'm not the way I think I should be, and I feel myself to be unlovable, what is there to be grateful for? My lack of gratitude in the present moment is another sign of my disconnection from myself and others, and from the world around me.

But then I notice that I have a beating heart. It began to beat and pump blood throughout my body, nourishing every cell with oxygen and other nutrients from the time I rested in my mother's womb. And it hasn't ceased beating for all of these years, no matter how I have felt about myself from one minute to the next. My brain, though scarred by the trauma of stress and burnout, is still carrying out all of its functions with amazing efficiency. The feelings that rise up from inside, though not always comfortable, don't go unnoticed. They inform me of my needs, and remind me to take care of myself. In touch with my own needs and feelings, I am able to connect with the needs and feelings of others. All of this is happening in the present moment. I am deeply grateful.

This experience of gratitude is so rich and fulfilling that I decide to continue. I think of the many people who played their part in my life perfectly, whether they were aware of it or not. Each of them was a teacher to me. Some taught me by becoming my mirror, showing me something about myself that I would not have otherwise discovered. The way they taught me was not always comfortable for me. Sometimes the learning process involved a lot of pain. Now, in the present moment, I am grateful for every teacher, every experience, and every lesson. I am deeply grateful.

I will not starve today. I have a roof over my head and a place to sleep. I have the tools I need to do my work. There is an entire universe of possibility at my fingertips. This present moment is a miracle of abundance.

Gratitude just taught me something new. The perfection I was seeking is already here. Everything is perfect in God, in this present moment. It just didn't look the way I expected it to.

By now I know myself well enough to recognize that gratitude will not come of its own accord and sweep me up in an ecstasy of thanksgiving. Gratitude is a friend who waits patiently for our meeting. It's up to me to shake off my complaining and grumbling and take the short walk to her door. Gratitude is something I must practice. I know one person who writes several pages every day in her journal, just expressing words of gratitude to God for everything. And I mean *everything*, even things that most of us would complain about. For her, every experience is a lesson, every person is a teacher, and everything is worthy of blessing. She didn't just wake up one day and become a grateful person. She practiced it until it transformed her.

When I am able to experience and express only gratitude for everything I have experienced: the light and the heavy, the easy and the difficult, the painful and the joyful, that's when I know I am open and receptive to the greatest of all gifts, the gift of love.

YOURS,

Tad

Letter Twenty: A Return to Love

DEAR BELOVED,

And now we return to love. The word love is thrown around so much in our society that it tends to lose its meaning. And as I mentioned in a previous letter, the English language doesn't do a very good job with love. There's romantic love. And erotic love. There's narcissistic self-love, something which is almost universally repulsive. In contrast, a healthy self-love is universally recognized as a necessity for a healthy life (only perfectionists miss that one!). And then there is agape love, the unconditional love which is selfless and eternal. Many odes to love (agape in Greek) have been written over the centuries, but one of the most beautiful and poignant is found in St. Paul's letter to the Corinthians: "Love is patient and kind; love does not envy or boast; it is not arrogant or rude. It does not insist on its own way; it is not irritable or resentful; it does not rejoice at wrongdoing, but rejoices with the truth. Love bears all things, believes all things, hopes all things, endures all things. Love never ends." The love described here, which St. Paul considers to be the character of Divine love and the model for loving human relations, is universally applicable. Applying all of the characteristics of love which he describes here in every relationship and every situation is the key to a life defined by love. And the relationship we must start with is the relationship with ourself. How we handle our own heart will determine how we handle the hearts of others.

If we want to live a life defined by love and know we must begin with ourselves, how do we handle our mind and heart when the thoughts and emotions—which were fostered by many years of a refusal to love and accept ourselves—return and cause us pain? If we've already done the hard work of forgiveness and learned the arts of vigilance and gratitude, the remainder of the healing depends on love. Everything we've discussed in the last few letters falls under the same banner. It's all about the care of the self. As we didn't learn to take care of ourselves in childhood, we had to experience the pain of self-abandonment. Now our very life depends on how well we learn the art of caring for ourselves.

We may recognize rationally that we are surrounded by people who love us (even if we can't understand why), and we may believe with all the faculties of our mind that that there is a Divine love "which surpasses all understanding," but if we don't take responsibility for the barriers to love which exist inside us, these *loves* will not be able to penetrate our heart. As the great poet Rumi wrote:

> *"Your task is not to seek for love, but merely to seek and find all the barriers within yourself that you have built against it."*

But how do we not only seek and find, but tear down and remove these barriers within? Let us return to the union of the mind and the heart. What our mind knows must be translated to the heart in a language it understands. The only language the heart speaks is *loving presence.* We must use the power of our mind and its presence in the heart to instill love there. Send compassion there, from the mind to the heart. Do it not once but continuously. In doing so you will break down the barriers to love, a love which does not flow only in one direction but like a wave of the great ocean flows in and out unceasingly.

YOURS,

Tad

Letter Twenty-one: Turning Our Love Outward

DEAR BELOVED,

I'd like to share with you something I have learned by experience. See if this is true in your own life. Perfectionists have a great capacity for empathy. The problem is, it's hidden under the layers of self-protection that build up as a result of entrenched perfectionism. Take yourself mentally back to the beginning of your perfectionism journey. How did it begin? Most likely, it began with an extraordinary level of sensitivity. Perhaps you took everything more seriously than your peers, were more sensitive to others' feelings, feared letting other people down, and blamed yourself for unfortunate events.

The burden of pain a young empath feels can become a burden of guilt, fear, and shame. Naturally, this young person doesn't want the pain to increase, so he tries to disconnect from this sensitivity. The need for security becomes paramount. Control is employed as a strategy to meet the need for security, and perfectionism is born. If this young person notices that the strategy is working in one area of his life, he may begin to apply it to other aspects as he matures. Underneath the hardened exterior of an abrasive perfectionist we often find a deeply sensitive person with a gift for empathy.

Once self-compassion has accomplished its share of healing work, the recovering perfectionist can once again turn his love outward. Longtime friends and acquaintances might even be amazed at the transformation. This person who once seemed to attack the world around him with the all the grace and subtlety of a wrecking ball is suddenly revealed to be open, present, compassionate and tolerant. The truth is, this gift for empathic connection was always present in the perfectionist, but they "decided" at some point early on (likely unconsciously) that the pain of connection was too much to bear in the absence of self-compassion.

From my experience I developed four "first principles" that I believe in and try to live by. Perhaps they will help you as well as you begin to turn your newfound love outward. Here they are:

No one is a finished product. Whether we realize it or not, we often limit ourselves and others by considering what we see today as a finished product. Signed, sealed, delivered, and static. We judge and behave as if this product were long ago processed, packaged and placed on the shelf, never to change for the better–and on the way to death and decomposition. We do this to ourselves and we do it to others. When we view others this way we are prone to criticize and judge them, and there is no room for empathy or presence. When we view ourselves this way, we give up and stop moving.

Each person's spiritual journey is a sacred and delicate thing. Compassion requires a humble approach. We don't have the right to burst into someone's life, point out their shortcomings and give them orders. The spiritual evolution of each soul occurs in its own time and is guided by a mystery we can't comprehend. What we can do is offer each person we meet the gift of our presence.

Everyone is doing the best they can. This is an assumption we can choose to make. If nothing else, it helps *us* to become softer and more tolerant. It makes empathy possible. Which makes compassion (suffering *with*) possible.

We are all connected to one another. When we emerge from the isolation of perfectionism and learn to be present with ourselves and others, we then begin to sense the equality and interconnectedness of all living beings. Self-compassion is not an end in itself. It is a vehicle of compassion which moves us beyond the self to a recognition of — and connection with — the Divine image reflected in each person, and every part of nature.

If we hold fast to these four "first principles" we will find that virtually all of our "interpersonal sins" will disappear on their own. Think about it: Where is room to be found for gossip, anger, slander, hatred or superiority if we follow these four basic rules of unconditional love? Giving ourselves and others the freedom to change, the room to grow, and the empathy to soften the bumps in the road is the beginning of an unconditional and all-encompassing love turned both inward and outward.

YOURS,

Tad

Letter Twenty-two: Today

DEAR BELOVED,

No matter how well we understand perfectionism, it can at any given moment appear as an intimidating monster. Perhaps that is because it is a monster with so many offspring. Depression, anxiety, the burden of shame, eating disorders, obsessive-compulsive thoughts, identity confusion, substance abuse, self-harm and thoughts of suicide–these are all the children of perfectionism, our refusal to love and accept ourselves in a state of imperfection. When they come to visit us as one monstrous family it can be overwhelming. We can't shoo them away with the brush of a hand. It's also difficult to treat them individually and ignore their common source, the refusal to love and accept ourselves in a state of imperfection.

Whether you understand all that I have written or need more of your own experience to verify my own reflections, it all comes down to today. As a perfectionist who has struggled to love and accept yourself for so long, you have been issued an invitation to a sacred pilgrimage. It's one of the most exquisite and fulfilling journeys you could ever hope to embark on. The destination is love, and the path runs through self-knowledge. We all recognize that whatever is handed to us on a silver platter, we tend to take for granted. When you reach your destination (though this journey never really ends) you will ascribe the highest value not only to the love you will have found, but to the self-knowledge you will have gained along the way. You will know you have reached your destination when you can say with total honesty "I am ready to kiss the feet of every one of my teachers (whether they be events or persons), thanking them for all the ways they helped me to learn to love myself and others, even if they had no idea what a beautiful mission they were fulfilling." What may seem like irrational gratitude to some is the hallmark of unconditional and boundless love for the one who had to *fight* for love and *suffer* for self-knowledge.

It all comes down to today. There will never be another day like today, and tomorrow is never guaranteed. What is the most loving thing you can do for yourself today? Finding the answer to this question will require getting in touch with your needs and feelings, and connecting the mind and heart. When this simple yet profound process of self-empathy becomes a habit, perfectionism and her offspring won't intimidate us nearly as much as they did before. When self-empathy becomes a habit, we will be much better equipped to answer the question: What's the most loving thing I can do for myself today? It may be a decision to treat my attention with respect, taking great care about the messages I allow to pass through my senses. It may be a decision to forgive myself for the failings of yesterday, or to forgive someone else so that I can move forward in a spirit of freedom. It may even be a decision to end my association with someone, thereby taking responsibility for my own well-being. It may be a decision to give my time and energy (of my own free will without coercion by shame) to help another and be 100 percent present for them. It may be a decision to fulfill my obligation to the best of my ability. It may be a decision to do all of these things in the coming days. The important thing is that I remain in a state of conscious harmony with all that I do, for I know the cost of unconsciously *doing*, and being driven by a need for the love and acceptance I so often refused myself. The decisions I take may not make sense to everyone. Some people may have gotten used to the perfectionist who out of shame or fear fulfilled their needs without any care for himself. They may seek explanations or try to regain control through the usual tactics. The only explanation I want to give in such a situation is this: "I did the most loving thing I could do for myself today. And I trust that this will open the possibility for love to do its work all around me, even if the ways of love are hard to comprehend."

It all comes down to today. Whatever I do today, I will do it from a place of love and care for myself. What about you?

YOURS,

Tad

Afterword

In March of 2017 I decided to begin a daily practice of writing. Writing is something I have always loved, but often neglected. When I did write, I hid my work away in a drawer. I began writing a novel, not really having any idea what I would do with it but enjoying the process. I never intended to write a non-fiction or self-help book. My writing habit was interrupted by a broken ankle, but soon I found myself writing about my personal experience with perfectionism. This book is one small part of all that I have written in recent months. I found the writing extremely therapeutic, and though I have always tended to be a very private person I finally decided that I should publish these reflections for the benefit of others.

Only after I had written most of this content did I stop to research the topic of perfectionism. Even then, I did not research the topic exhaustively. As this book is part memoir, I was primarily concerned with writing *my truth,* not a textbook or a traditional product of research. What I did notice in the more recent publications is the growing awareness of perfectionism as a root problem of a number of disorders and other problems. This only confirmed my experience of perfectionism as an holistic problem which requires an holistic approach.

The union of the mind and heart in prayer and contemplation is an important concept in Eastern Christianity, one which stands at the center of the early Christian mystical tradition. This may be surprising to some who are under the impression that Christianity does not teach any form of mindful prayer. The practice of uniting the mind and the heart in Eastern Christianity makes use of a single prayer which is repeated continuously: "Lord Jesus Christ, have mercy on me." Christian readers of this book can easily find more information about this form of prayer simply by searching for "Jesus Prayer." There are many volumes available on this topic. Because I intended for the contents of this book to be accessible to all, no matter their creed or culture, I adapted the powerful concept of the union of the mind and the heart in a more general way here. What's especially interesting to me is that science is now confirming the ancient teachings about the power of the mind and the heart.

Some may be disappointed by the general (non-dogmatic) spiritual tone of my reflections. What I believe is what I wrote, that the spiritual evolution of each and every person is a sacred and delicate matter. If I am able to help even one person remove the barriers to love from his or her heart through what I have written here, I will be immensely grateful.

Please write to me at tad@tadfrizzell.com and let me know why you chose this book, and how perfectionism has affected your life. I would love to hear from you.

* * *

For more resources on the topics described in this book, please visit www.tadfrizzell.com and click the tab labeled "Resources".

Urgent Request

Thank you for reading my book!

I really appreciate feedback, and I would love to hear what you have to say about it. I need your input to make my next version of the book and all my future books better.

Please leave a helpful review on Amazon and let me know your reaction to the book. Leaving a review is one of the best ways you can help others who need help with their perfectionism to find it.

Acknowledgments

I would like to thank Judith Oakland for agreeing to be the first reader of this book, and for her encouragement to publish. I am grateful to the new friends I have found through the Self-Publishing School Mastermind Community who are constantly supporting one another on the path to writing and publishing. This book was written with love and gratitude to all those who have pushed me onward through fear and doubt. Thank you.

About the Author

Tad Frizzell is a bestselling author whose life has been filled with mountains, monasteries, and travels in foreign lands. He writes to navigate the wilderness which is the human heart. Visit his website for more information.

Get in touch:

www.tadfrizzell.com
tad@tadfrizzell.com

Made in the USA
Lexington, KY
25 February 2018